Princeton University

Replies of the Professors and Tutors of Princeton College

To the Questions Addressed to Them by the Board of Trustees

Princeton University

Replies of the Professors and Tutors of Princeton College
To the Questions Addressed to Them by the Board of Trustees

ISBN/EAN: 9783337171339

Printed in Europe, USA, Canada, Australia, Japan

Cover: Foto ©ninafisch / pixelio.de

More available books at **www.hansebooks.com**

REPLIES

OF THE

Professors and Tutors of Princeton College

TO THE

QUESTIONS ADDRESSED TO THEM

BY THE

BOARD OF TRUSTEES.

1881.

ELIZABETH, N. J.:
Journal Printing House, Cor. Broad and Jersey Streets.
1881.

INDEX.

iii.

QUESTIONS

ADDRESSED BY

The Board of Trustees to the Several Professors of the College of New Jersey.

I. What in detail are the special topics taught in your department or departments?

II. How many hours a week are you employed in giving instruction to your class or classes?

III. What proportion of these hours do you give respectively to lectures and to recitations?

IV. Do you use a text-book or text-books, and if so, what?

V. Do you require any written exercises from the students in your class or classes? If so, what are they, and how many during the year?

VI. Do you give any instruction to pupils in addition to what you give in the recitation room? If so, please specify its nature.

VII. Do you have any laboratory work with the students? If so, what in? If your department does not admit of that, do you have any sort of exercises corresponding to laboratory work?

VIII. Have you any suggestions to make for the improvement of your department, which, in your judgment, the Trustees would do well to carry out?

IX. Have you, during the past year, published any book, pamphlet, monograph, or article in a Review on the special branch which you teach, or on any other branch? If so, give the title or titles.

iv.

JAMES McCOSH, D.D., LL. D.,

President,

And Robert Lenox Professor of Biblical Instruction.

Query I. I give instruction in Four Departments:

I. PSYCHOLOGY.

To the Juniors. I begin with explaining the Method of Inquiry which is that of Induction with Consciousness as the main instrument of Observation. I deliver some lectures on Mind and Body. I show that mind exists, and give an introduction to the study. I classify the powers of the mind:

First Group—The Cognitive. Second Group—The Motive.

    I. Simple Cognitive or Presentative.

    II. Reproductive or Representative.

    III. Comparative, which Discover Relations.

    IV. Moral Power or Conscience.

    V. Emotions

    VI. Will or Optative.

I unfold the method of operation and laws of each of these powers:

The 1st embraces—(1) Sense Perception. (2) Self Consciousness.

2d. (1) The Relentive. (2) The Recalling (Phantasy). (3) Association of Ideas. (4) Recognitive (the main element in Memory). (5) The Compositive (the main element in Imagination). (6) The Symbolic (the main element in Language).

3d. The Faculty which discovers Relations which are classified—(1) Identity. (2) Whole and Parts. (3) Resemblance. (4) Space. (5) Time. (6) Quantity. (7) Active Property. (8) Cause and Effect.

4th. The Conscience, which is both a Cognitive and a Motive Power. It reveals certain great truths. It is treated of in its development and growth, and its actual operations.

5th. The Emotions embrace an Appetence, an Idea, Excitement with Attachment and Repugnance, and an Organic Affection.

6th. The essence of Will is Choice, and it has influence over all the other powers of the mind.

II. The History of Philosophy.

To an Elective Class of Seniors. The Rise of Philosophy. A classification of the various Mental Sciences. Most of the First Term occupied with the Ancient Greek Philosophy. An account is given of the Pre-Socratic Schools—Ionic, Pythagorean, Eleatic; of Anaxagoras, Heraclitus, Empedocles and Democritus; of the Sophists, Socrates, Plato, Aristotle; the Stoics, Epicureans and Alexandrians. This occupies the First Term. I begin the Second Term with a lecture or two on the Medieval Philosophy, and then give a critical account of the systems of Bacon; Descartes; Spinoza; Locke; Berkeley; the Scottish School; Hume; Reid; the German School; Leibnitz; Kant; the French Schools; Hamilton; Mill.

III. Discussions in Contemporary Philosophy.

To a Post Graduate Class. In this class the leading philosophic questions of the day are discussed, such as Agnosticism; Criteria of different kinds of Truth, First Truths, Reasoned Truths, Inductive Truths; Mind and Body; Materialism; Development; Cause and Effect; The Theistic Arguments; The Growth of Conscience; Moral Good; The German Philosophy; Kant; Herbert Spencer.

IV. Biblical Instruction.

To Senior Class, Academic and Scientific, I deliver a series of short papers on the Pentateuch, and have recitations on these and on chapters read. I endeavor to clear up the difficulties connected with the ancient books, and point out the harmony between Genesis and Geology. I unfold the grand truths revealed in the Books of Moses, especially those relating to the Providence of God and the promised Messiah. This occupies the First Term. In the Second and Third Terms, I expound and have recitations on the first eight chapters of the Epistle to the Romans, and give a brief exposition and defence of the leading doctrines of Scripture, such as the Existence of God, the Immortality of the Soul, Sin, Redemption, Justification, Faith, Repentance, Love, Good Works, Reconciliation of Paul and James, Sanctification.

Query II. I have four lectures or recitations every week; and each of these implies preparatory work. I calculate that I devote another hour a week to preaching, to addresses at prayer meetings and other meetings of students. My duties as President do not allow of my giving more time to teaching.

Query III. In each of my classes I first give two lectures carefully prepared, and then have a recitation upon them at the following meeting. In the Post Graduate Class this recitation takes the form of a discussion.

Query IV. In the Department of Psychology, I constantly refer to my work on the "Intuitions," and in the History of Philosophy to Ueberweg's History. In the Discussions on Contemporary Philosophy, I refer to books and papers on the subjects treated. In the religious instruction, the Pentateuch and the Epistle to the Romans are my text books. In all my classes I refer to works which I recommend my students to read.

Queries V, VI, and VII. I have from time to time a meeting in my Library, open to all the members of the Junior and Senior Classes, for the discussion of philosophic themes; and there an essay is read commonly by a Post Graduate student or an Alumnus, and remarks are made upon it and upon the subject of the essay. In all my classes I encourage reading, and give an opportunity to the students to use the results of their reading.

Query VIII. I am of opinion that in our College the physical sciences in which we have thirteen instructors are beginning to overshadow the philosophical departments which have hitherto occupied so high a place in Princeton College. I hope that we may be able to devise a plan by which the mental and moral sciences may be able to maintain their place alongside of the literary and scientific branches.

Query IX. I have published an article on "Agnos-

8

ticism as developed in Huxley's Hume" in Popular Science Monthly, August, 1879; an article on "Joseph Cook" in the Catholic Presbyterian, September, 1879; an article on "Herbert Spencer's Ethics" in the Princeton Review, November, 1879; a book on the "Emotions" in January, 1880; an article on "The Development and Growth of Conscience" in the Princeton Review, July, 1880; a paper on "Harmonizing the action of the Primary, the Secondary, and the Collegiate systems of, *Education*," read before the National Association of Teachers in July, 1880, and published in the new Journal Education; an article on "A Presbyterian College in America" in Catholic Presbyterian, August, 1880; a paper on "How we are to deal with young men trained in natural science in this age of unsettled opinion," read before the Presbyterian Council in Philadelphia, September, 1880; and an article on "The Criteria of various kinds of truth" in the Princeton Review, November, 1880.

LYMAN H. ATWATER, D.D., LL. D.,

Professor of Logic and Moral and Political Science.

I. The topics taught by me are Logic, Metaphysics, Ethics, Economics and Political Science, including International Law.

II. Five hours with classes in the class room, and more when I meet them in divisions. Several hours in immediate preparation for them, over and above general studies in the branches specified. Five, or the equivalent of five hours per week in the labor involved in examining and grading my classes.

III. I divide my time about equally between lectures and recitations, being of opinion that lectures not thoroughly recited upon can accomplish little.

IV. I use my own Manual of Logic, Woolsey's International Law, and recommend books to be consulted along with my lectures. I am considering the expediency of a further use of text-books.

10

V. I require usually three written examinations from the Junior, and two from the Senior Class.

VI. I give aid to students seeking light in my own and collateral departments by personal expositions, and by guiding their reading.

VII. None except work upon the black-board.

VIII. That depends upon what it might appear that the Trustees have the means and disposition to do. The examination of classes numbering 260, all about the same time, is very onerous. I have the Junior and Senior Classes, each numbering over 90, and an Elective Class (volunteer on my part, because I saw no other provision for it), numbering 75.

IX. I published during the past year in the Princeton Review an article largely ethical, entitled "The a priori Novum Organum of Christianity;" another entitled, "Political Economy a Science—of what?" an article in the Catholic Presbyterian entitled "Prof. Calderwood's Contributions to Philosophy;" a revised edition of my "Manual of Logic;" some smaller contributions to weekly papers on "Broad-Churchism," "Conscience and Evolution," "Herbert Spencer's Principia of Ethics;" Critiques on several Theological and Economic Works in the Presbyterian Review; and have now in press a paper read before the recent Presbyterian Council on "Religion and Politics."

I deem it, however, simply just to state, that my time is so much occupied by extra-professorial work committed to me by the authorities of the College, that I find it hard to seize even snatches of time to work up an important article which I have commenced. Besides

11

attendance on faculty meetings and committees, ordinary and extraordinary, I have long been class-officer, and superintendent of the whole department of gratuitous aid to the students, each of which offices involves a consumption of time and strength best known to those who try them. Of late, also, I have been made chairman of the Faculty Sanitary Committee, the duties of which have been quite heavy thus far. I hope they will be less so hereafter. I might mention other College demands upon my time, but perhaps I have specified enough to explain, if explanation be needed, why my publications have not been more numerous.

ARNOLD GUYOT, Ph.D., LL. D.,

Blair Professor of Geology and Physical Geography.

I. The Department entrusted to me has thus far comprised " Geology and Physical Geography, or the Science of the Earth, including the Life System, in its past and its present condition."

II. The instruction has been given to the Junior and Senior Classes in two alternate courses of lectures, one on Geology and the other on Physical Geography, composed each of about 120 exercises, exclusive of examinations, which consumed 30 hours more.

III. The recitations occupied from one quarter to one-fifth of the whole time.

IV. No text-books have been used, but several were recommended for private study.

V. By my original contract all my teaching was to be concentrated within six months, in order to leave me time for investigations and publications, a feature which was considered an advantage to the College. After my illness in 1870, and since 1872, my teaching time, by a new arrangement, was reduced one-half which was to be applied to Physical Geography only. But no suitable person having been found to take up the course of Geology, I assumed again that portion of my department. The work of preparation thus remained the same as previously, but the time allotted to each course having become too short for the subject to be taught, I was obliged to drop the recitations and to replace them by an extensive written examination at mid-term, and an oral one at the end of the course; both together consuming for the two classes, from 60 to 70 hours. Thanks to the election of an Assistant in Geology, though the number of my teaching hours remains the same, I shall henceforth be relieved of the preparatory work for, and teaching of, Geology, and I shall be able to divide the Senior Class, a change which is much to be desired.

VI. I do not give any regular instruction outside of the recitation room, but have occasionally answered the request of my class to deliver some extra lectures, such as on "Genesis and Geology;" "The place of Man in the System of Life;" "The place of America in Universal History," &c.

VII. The Museum Work in Geology has mostly been entrusted to Prof. Hill, under my direction.

I may be permitted here to say that since the foundation of the E. M. Museum by the munificence of an honored friend of the College, the building up and the direction of that noble Institution, added to my present teaching duties, have required a share of my time and strength full as great as that which I have devoted to the College at any period of my connection with it.

VIII. My course of Physical Geography, as I had marked it out, comprises two distinct parts: Physical Geography proper, and a second, treating of the Earth

14

as the abode of man; Primeval man and the human races; the influence of Physical Geography, viz., of geographical forms and climate, on the development of the human races, their migrations, the course of history, and kindred topics. The limited time never allowed me to develop the second, the most important and philosophical part, in any way satisfactory to myself, and worthy of a final College course. I would consider it a great improvement in our curriculum if, at some future time, the first part, or physical geography proper, should be taught, with my Physical Geography as a text-book, by some younger man, in the lower classes, as preparatory for the course of Geology, while the second, more historical part, would be reserved for my course in the Senior Class, as a crowning philosophical study, combining nature and the history and progress of the human race.

IX. As my extraneous work was, in some measure, a part of my engagement, I beg leave to recall the manner in which I have performed it.

In 1859, I finished the large volume of Meteorological and Physical tables, published by the Smithsonian Institute. Since 1862 to this day, I have issued successively seven volumes of my series of Geographies, containing much over a hundred and fifty maps, together with thirty original wall maps, physical and classical. I wrote the Treatise on Physical Geography at the head of Johnson's Atlas. I was with President Barnard of Columbia College, co-director of, and contributor to, Johnson's Encyclopedia. I wrote an essay on the Biblical account of Creation and Modern Science for

15

the Evangelical Alliance Volume in 1873. I have delivered a number of courses of over twenty each, lectures on Geology and Genesis, on Ethnology, on the Functions of the Various Races of Men in History and similar subjects, in the Theological Seminary of this place; two courses, of twelve lectures each, on Creation according to the Bible and Modern Science, and on Primeval Man, in Union Theological Seminary (Morse foundation;) one on Man and Human Races in Hartford Theological Seminary; another on the Unity and Variety of the System of Life at the Smithsonian Institute; one also at the Brooklyn Institute, on the Graham foundation.

I have contributed various partly unpublished papers, almost one a year, to the National Academy of Science since its foundation.

My vacations have been mostly devoted to the investigations of the Physical Structure of the Appalachian System of Mountains, the results of which are partly printed in two preliminary papers in Silliman's American Journal of Science, one in 1861, the other in 1880, the last with a map of the Catskill Mountains. Another larger original map of the Catskills is published separately. A map of the Mountain System of North Carolina, surveyed by myself, with the measurement of nearly 700 mountains, is still in manuscript. Altogether my mountain measurements, from Maine to Georgia, amount to over a thousand.

JOHN T. DUFFIELD, D.D.,

Dod Professor of Mathematics.

I. The following subjects are taught in the Mathematical Department: Algebra, Geometry, and Mensuration in the Freshman year; Plane Trigonometry, Navigation, Surveying, Spherical Trigonometry and Elementary Analytical Geometry in the Sophomore year; Analytical Geometry of two dimensions completed, Analytical Geometry of three dimensions, and the Differential and Integral Calculus in the Junior and Senior years.

II. I am occupied nine hours a week in the Class-room—six hours with the Sophomore Class, two hours with the Junior, and one hour with the Senior.

III. At the commencement of each of the main branches of study, I give an Introductory Lecture on the subject, and at each exercise with the class I occupy a portion of the time in oral instruction.

IV. The Text-Book in Algebra is Ray's University Algebra; in Geometry, Todhunter's Euclid—supplemented by original Propositions given by the Instructor. Mensuration in the Freshman year is for the present taught without a Text-Book.

17

In the other branches of Mathematics, we use Loomis' Series of Text-Books, accompanied by oral instruction. This feature of our method of instruction is so prominent that it might be more correct to say, that in our College the branches of Mathematics just referred to are taught mainly by Lecture—the Text-Books being used by way of reference, and as furnishing examples for practice. The students are required to take notes of the Lectures, and submit their note-books for examination at the end of each Term.

V. Throughout the course at almost every recitation I give as an optional exercise Questions and Problems not contained in the Text-Book, the answers or solutions to be given in writing. Students who present solutions are liable to be called on to give the solutions at the black-board.

VI, VII. I have no formal arrangement for instruction in addition to that given in the Class-room.

VIII. I propose giving to the Senior Elective Class a short course of Lectures on Quaternions. With this exception, I should not at present recommend any change in our course of instruction in Mathematics. It is the ordinary College course, and could not be materially extended without increasing the time allotted to Elective Studies, or increasing the requirement for admission. In view of the inadequate provision for thorough instruction in the Mathematics of our Freshman year in most of the schools where our students are prepared for College, I doubt whether any advance in our requirement for admission would be advisable.

IX. With the exception of a few newspaper articles,

18

I have published nothing within the past year. I have for some time had it in mind to prepare and publish a series of Text-Books on Trigonometry, Analytical Geometry, and the Calculus, embodying the results of my experience in teaching these branches. I have not done so, mainly owing to the state of my health, which has prevented me from undertaking much work outside of my ordinary College duties.

P. S.—Understanding the first question to refer to the studies of the Curriculum, I have replied as above. It gives me pleasure to add that the Assistant in Mathematics, who has given special attention to the Modern Higher Algebra and Geometry, has a Post-Graduate Class in these branches.

J. STILLWELL SCHANCK, M.D., LL. D.,

Professor of Chemistry.

I. (*a*) General Chemistry; also Galvanism, Electro-Magnetism, &c., including Applications such as Telegraph, &c. (required).

(*b*) Applied Chemistry and Organic Chemistry (elective).

(*c*) Human Anatomy and Physiology.

II. First term, five hours; second and third terms always three, sometimes four.

III. Not more than one-fifth or one-sixth of my exercises are recitations.

These need some comment. Chemistry to-day is a very extensive subject, and its applications are everywhere and constant. It requires severe compression to introduce what should be presented in the lecture hours at my disposal. The course could be improved and more recitations introduced if more time could be had. My course of instruction is very fully illustrated by experiments. I estimate that each lecture needs four hours or more of time.

IV. Roscoe's Chemistry or Fowne's Chemistry, or both.

V. Two elaborate written examinations, and in

20

Chemistry sometimes a written paper at the end of second term sometimes not, for want of time.

VI. Much conversational and explanatory instruction is given after lecture to groups around the table during the year.

VII. Six or eight years ago I made several elaborate annual trials of Laboratory experimenting by the class. It usually began well, but soon became irksome, more frequently failed for want of time or want of knack, or of cleanliness. The necessary expense was an item with some, and the accommodations (basement of N. C.) too dark and uninviting. Much time was consumed and really but little accomplished. In lieu of this, some work is now done in the Analytical Laboratory under Prof. Cornwall or his Assistant. Experimenting as above is also renewed this year by a few.

VIII. An additional hour per week for Chemistry would result in a fuller and better course. But that would be at the expense of some other department. The branches now taught are very numerous. Chemistry probably has its full share of time.

Anatomy and Physiology I teach two hours per week to two divisions (one hour each) of the Sophomore Class during first term. This excites interest and close attention. If a few hours more could be devoted to these subjects so as to amplify a little more and introduce more of health and hygiene, the course would be improved and the students gratified.

IX. I regret to say that I am not conscious of having known much of anything during the past year worthy of publication that I had not reason to believe was equally well known by others.

HENRY C. CAMERON, Ph.D., D.D.,

Professor of Greek Language and Literature.

I. Greek Language and Literature.
  (*a*) Senior Class. Tragedy and Greek Literature.
  (*b*) Junior Class. Tragedy and History.
  (*c*) Sophomore Class. Epic Poetry.
  (*d*) Freshman Class. Oratory.

II. Senior Class, one hour; Junior Class, two hours; Sophomore Class, four hours; Freshman Class, two hours.

III. Senior Class, one-fourth of the time to Lectures, three-fourths to Recitations; Junior Class, one-fourth to Lectures or Prolegomena, three-fourths to Recitations; Sophomore and Freshman Classes, no formal lectures except at the opening and close of the course in explanation of the language and dialects, and the "Homeric Question," &c. All matters pertaining to mythology, history, antiquities, &c., are explained in connection with the recitations.

IV. Senior Class, Crosby's or any edition of the Œdipus Tyrannus; Junior Class, Harper's Text of the

Medea of Euripides, Owen's Thucydides; Sophomore Class, Owen's Iliad of Homer; Freshman Class, Stevens' Orations of Lysias.

V. Written Examinations several times a year.

VI. No formal instruction, but advice as to reading, &c.

VII. None.

VIII. A Museum containing models of the Parthenon, the Acropolis, a Greek Theatre, Copies of the Elgin and other collections, casts of the finest statues, and two more sets of the Ancient Maps by Prof. Guyot and myself.

IX. Reminiscences of Prof. Henry; Sermon on Jonathan Dickinson.

CHARLES W. SHIELDS, D.D., LL.D.,

Professor of History and of the Harmony of Science and Revealed Religion.

The Department of the Harmony of Science and Revealed Religion extends through the Junior and Senior years, and embraces the following topics :

Junior First Term—Natural Theology and the Physical Sciences; Existence of a First Cause; Personality of the First Cause; Attributes of the Divine Person, as illustrated by Astronomy, Geology, and Anthropology.

Junior Second Term—Natural Religion and the Mental Sciences; Problem of a Future Life, of a Divine Government, Probation, Theodicy, as illustrated by Psychology, Sociology, and Natural Theology.

Senior First Term—Christian Evidences and Inductive Logic; Probability of a Supernatural Revelation; History, Classification and Value of its Evidences; Miraculous, Prophetical, Historical and Scientific Evidences; History, Classification and Methods of the Sciences; Logical Rules for correlating Reason and Revelation in the Scale of the Sciences.

Senior Second Term—Christian Science and Philosophy; History of Christian Science; Existing Parties in Christian Science; Religious Problems in the Sciences;

Existing and Prospective Harmony of Revealed Religion with the Physical Sciences; with the Psychical Sciences; the issuing Final Philosophy.

The Department of History extends through the Junior and Senior years, and embraces the following topics:

Junior First Term—Primitive European Civilization; its Elements and Characteristics; the Barbarian Period; the Feudal Period; the Christian Church.

Junior Second Term—Mediæval European Civilization; the Theocratic Period; the Monarchical Period; Democratic Institutions; the Reformation; the English, French and American Revolutions.

. Senior First Term—English and American Civilization; English Institutions under Henry VII; Religious and Political Parties; the Commonwealth; the Restoration; Scottish Institutions; Elements of American Civilization; the Colonial Period; the Revolutionary Period; the Constitutional Period; the Period of Political Development; Critical Epoch of Civil War; Problems and Tendencies of American Civilization.

Senior Second Term—Ancient and Modern Civilization; Characteristics of Universal Civilization; the Primitive Civilizations of Asia, Africa, Europe and America; Jewish Period of the Pre-Christian Civilization; Roman Period; the Formative Period of Christian Civilization; Experimental Period; Modern Progressive Period; Problems and Tendencies of Christian Civilization.

Schools of Philosophical History. Conditions and Prospects of a Science of History.

Four hours a week throughout the year are devoted

25

to these courses of instruction; two in each Department.

Two of these hours are devoted to lectures, and two to recitations; a lecture and a recitation in each Department.

The text-books used in History are Guizot's History of European Civilization, and Hallam's Constitutional History of England; those used in the Harmony of Science and Religion are Paley's Natural Theology and Butler's Analogy of Religion.

Five or six written examinations are held annually, each providing for an extemporaneous essay upon the topics of the preceding course.

Within these Departments are also included the Dickenson Prize Essay, the Science and Religion Prize Essay, and the Boudinot Historical Fellowship.

All instruction is given publicly to the whole class, with a standing invitation to come to the Professor for private explanations, which, however, are not allowed to interfere with a fair competition for grades, honors and prizes.

WILLIAM A. PACKARD, Ph.D.,

Kennedy Professor of Latin Language and Literature and the Science of Language.

I. Latin Language and Literature and Science of Language. Instruction in this Department involves,

First.—The constant training of classes in the Etymology and Syntax of the language, and in the power to translate it accurately and fluently into idiomatic English.

Second.—The reading and interpretation of particular authors, whether literary or historical, or both combined. This implies, as collateral branches of study, the History of Roman Literature and the Archæology of Roman Life, social and political. Roman History is studied in its three leading periods: First, in connection with portions of Livy's Histories, the early history down to the times of the Gracchi; second, in connection with Cicero's Letters, the period from the Gracchi to the Empire; and, third, in connection with Juvenal's Satires and Pliny's Letters, the earlier

27

Empire, especially its moral and religious aspects in contrast with Christian Truth and Christian Life. The Science of Language is treated in lectures upon its General Principles; Physiology and Mechanism of Speech; Phonetic Laws; Formation of Words; History of Inflections; Comparative Laws of Syntax.

II. Ten hours weekly as the average, sometimes more, as follows:

Freshmen in three divisions during three-quarters of the year.

Sophomores in two divisions, three hours weekly through the year.

Juniors (elective), two hours, two-thirds of the year. (Voluntary evening class one to two hours).

Seniors (elective), one hour through the year. Voluntary one to two).

Post-Graduate, one to two hours through the year.

III. My exercises with the two lower classes are chiefly recitations, accompanied, or rather interspersed with constant communication of collateral illustrative instruction suggested by the text-book, calculated to quicken and broaden the interest of the student, with care, however, not to infringe upon the frequency and thoroughness of the recitations required of the student. Occasional lectures of a more formal character are introduced in the Sophomore year. These treat, in connection with Cicero's Letters, the representative characters and historical scenes and topics there found; and in connection with Horace, the History of Literature down to his time; his contemporaries, the introduction and influence of Greek, especially Alexandrian litera-

28

ture at Rome, and his own characteristics as to topics, style, views of life, &c.

In the Junior year my lectures are more frequent; in connection with Juvenal and Pliny treating of the other sources of our more intimate knowledge of the social and moral condition of the Empire in Italy and the Provinces; and, in connection with such of Cicero's rhetorical, ethical or religious treatises as I read with students, treating of the literary life and training at Rome, the sources and character of Roman Philosophy, and the Religion of Rome. In the Senior year my lectures occupy about one-third of the time, being in part illustrative of Lucretius, but chiefly upon the Science of Language.

IV. I state the authors used by me in the order of my curriculum: Horace's Odes; Selected Letters of Cicero (my own selection); Horace's Satires and Epistles; Juvenal's Satires and Selected Letters of Pliny; Cicero's Treatises (De Oratore, De Natura Deorum, De Fato, &c., varying from year to year); Lucretius De Rerum Natura; Bruns, Fontes Juris Romanæ, with use of Corpus Inscriptionum Latinarum and Ritschl, Priscæ Latinitatis Monumenta.

V. I suggest questions for special investigation, and designate volumes and parts of volumes, illustrative of the author or period under study, to be read in private by the class during the term, upon which questions are put in my examination papers eliciting extended written answers. All my examinations are in writing.

VI. I have a voluntary class of Juniors, and propose one of Seniors, each, weekly, one to two hours in the evening at my study. The Juniors are reading at present Cicero De Oratore. For the Seniors I take the topic of early Roman Laws and Epigraphic Remains. Works like Maine's Ancient Law and De Coulange's La Cité Antique cover the prehistoric ground, and form introductory and collateral reading.

VII. The work above indicated may be regarded as the answer to this question, with the addition of exercises in extemporaneous translation and interpretation of passages at sight, both oral and written.

VIII. The Department seems to me in a satisfactory condition.

IX. An article in the Presbyterian Review entitled, Juvenal's Historical Judgments; some Literary Notices; Sketches of College Presidents in the Princeton Book.

JOSEPH KARGÉ, Ph.D.,

Woodhull Professor of Continental Languages and Literature.

I. French and German grammar, reading, oral and written translations from original idioms into English and vice versa; practical application of these languages in using them as vehicles of explanation and illustration. History of gradual development of each, kinship to others on the European continent, intellectual treasures of their literature, and influence exercised in elevating the standard of modern civilization.

II. Number of hours devoted to class instruction varies with the number of students. The present Sophomores, of whom French is required throughout the year, have two hours per week. Average number of students in attendance one hundred and four.

Saturday being the only day in the week on which the class can meet the instructor in divisions of twenty-five students each without interfering with other departments, the method of instruction is both oral and written, the latter on the black board, in which the

31

entire division engages at the same time, illustrating and putting into practice rules previously explained; special pains being taken that each student draws from his own resources. In this manner, the preliminary rules of the language are thoroughly inculcated. Individual reading, parsing, translation and rapid manipulation of the verb in connection with sentences and periods strictly adhered to.

Tuesdays, when other departments claim the attention of the class, two divisions only, averaging fifty each, meet the instructor. The lesson is devoted to a recapitulation of what has been practiced on the previous Saturday, by turning rapidly into French, after dictation, English themes carefully arranged for that occasion by the teacher. At the close of an hour, all papers are taken up and carefully examined by the instructor in his study, mistakes underscored and returned to the pupil for correction and written explanation. This method, laborious as it will be seen, has proved by long experience the most effective, both in theoretical and practical results, besides keeping up an ever increasing interest and emulation of a large majority in the class. Number of hours per week devoted to the Sophomores averages between sixteen and eighteen, viz.: Six hours, in the class room; eight to ten hours in looking over written recitations and reviewing corrections; two hours, in coaching students, who either through sickness or other causes have been prevented from class attendance.

Juniors—There are a certain number of studies left to the choice of the student in the two upper classes, the Continental languages being included. Any student

32

enrolling his name for the continuance of French in the Junior class is compelled to take also German; two hours per week being allotted to both. The essential preliminaries having been mastered in the previous class, a course of reading in French is taken up, consisting of the choicest pieces of the classical drama, viz.: "Le Cid," of Corneille; "L'Athalie," of Racine; "Les Fourberies de Scapin," of Moliere. In reading these critically, both grammar and practical application are steadily kept in view. Besides, questions are made in the language taught, and answers in the same language insisted upon by the instructor.

The German language being a new study, the method pursued with it is essentially the same as in the Sophomore class in French, except that during the first term written recitations are suspended and in lieu thereof written exercises are insisted upon once a week, to enable the students to acquire sufficient practice in forming written characters. Meantime, great attention is paid to grammar and the acquisition of a vocabulary, so that at the beginning of the second term, a reader can be placed in the hands of the pupils and the course of weekly recitations resumed, which continue to the close of the academic year.

Average time devoted to this class is ten hours per week, viz.: To two divisions, forty each, four hours; four hours in looking over written recitations, and from one to two hours with students who require additional assistance outside of the class room.

Seniors—The number of electives in this class decreases about twenty per cent., and consequently the labor of instruction becomes less onerous. It is optional

33

with the student to take either one or both of the languages; the majority, however, show a decided preference for the German; the proportion in the present class being forty-two, among sixty-five electives; five take both. One hour per week is assigned to each. As considerable preliminary work still remains to be done in German to fit the student for an intelligent and extensive course of reading, this class meets the instructor in two divisions, twenty-one each. To familiarize the student with the intricacies of the German style, historical prose is selected, and after a fair mastery of the same, choice pieces of an epic, lyric and dramatic nature from Lessing, Schiller and Goethe are read, with critical analysis of characters, bringing also to the notice of the student their ethical and esthetical tendencies. The French course is essentially the same, except the students having had better opportunities to familiarize themselves with that language, and knowing Latin, a more comprehensive insight into the history of its growth and development is afforded them. At the middle of the second term, although a part of the time is still employed in the practical acquisition of these languages, the other part is devoted to lectures. A cursory view is taken:

(*a*) Of the Ethnology of Europe

(*b*) Of the literary nations constituting the Aryan stock.

(*c*) European families springing from that stock.

(*d*) Geographical distribution of these families.

(*e*) Physical, moral, and political causes which have operated to advance or retard their intellectual growth.

(*f*) Degree of kinship existing between them, illustrated by linguistic comparisons.

(*g*) Origin of modern nations emanating from each of the three great families, and the rank they occupy in the realm of modern letters.

Of the literary treasures of France and Germany a comprehensive exposition is given, tracing from the traditional and legendary periods the gradual development in letters to the classical period. Eminent writers of the same are reviewed with reference to salient traits, showing the influence which they have exerted upon contemporary and succeeding generations.

IV. Text-books in this department are indispensable to the pupil, but seldom or never made use of by the teacher in the class-room; principles being conveyed by means of oral and written exercises. To secure unity of plan among the instructors in this department, weekly conférences are held, in which suggestions and comparisons are made and results noted.

Before concluding the questions referring to the Academic Department, it is proper to add, that the French language is made a required study in the Freshman class during the last term of the year. The class is taught in divisions as in succeeding years. Additional time amounts to eight hours class instruction per week, besides a like number of hours for looking over written recitations.

Questions *III*, *V* and *VI* are included in the answer given to question *II*.

SCHOOL OF SCIENCE.

The same method is pursued here as above, except that in the two lower classes the oral mode of instruction proves more effective, owing to the limited number of students in a class room. To test the progress and practical knowledge of the students, written recitations take place every two weeks. Six hours in the Freshman and four hours in the Sophomore class per week are allowed for both these languages. During the first two years the instructors aim rather to obtain the largest possible amount of practical than technical knowledge, for the purpose of enabling the student when in the Junior class to seek information in French and German authors on scientific subjects involving original research.

In the two upper classes three hours are devoted to the study of languages. The want of an efficient assistant in past time has been felt, consequently the instructors are obliged to confine themselves for the current year to a curriculum which ought to have been completed in the two lower classes. Henceforth, it will be the earnest endeavor to thoroughly ground the pupils in the preliminaries, for which the first two years afford sufficient opportunity. The two succeeding years will be devoted to a literary course in which the student will be led to a higher appreciation of the languages. As means of conveyance the languages taught are to be used altogether, and written exercises, compositions and themes bearing on scientific subjects will be required.

To supply material for compositions and themes, a scientific compendium in French and German is in preparation, and will be introduced at an early day, embracing the history of the most important inventions and discoveries; also extracts from noted authorities.

VIII. In the way of suggestion, I would respectfully ask that more opportunity be given to the students of the College of New Jersey for the study of German. The present allowance barely averages sixty-eight hours in a course of two academic years; while a three-fold amount would be none too much. The desire for the acquisition of this language has been steadily on the increase, and I am justified in saying that in spite of the limited time given to it, the results are gratifying, owing chiefly to the zest which the students evince for its mastery.

IX. The instructors in this department, however ambitious to crystallize the substance of their experience in the form of publications, are taxed to the utmost limits, and the time remaining to their disposal barely suffices to keep them posted on the current topics of their own department.

RECAPITULATION.

The exact number of students attending this department is as follows:

Sophomore, Academic, required, one hundred
and four - - - - - - - (104)
Juniors, Elective, eighty - - - - - (80)
Seniors,   "   sixty - - - - - (60)
Freshmen, required, during the last term of the
year, one hundred - - - - - (100)

Scientific Seniors, seven - - - - - (7)
    "   Juniors, eight - - - - - (8)
    "   Sophomores, twenty - - - - (20)
    "   Freshmen, eighteen - - - - (18)

Grand total, - - - - 397

Total of hours of class room instruction per week during the first two terms, twenty-nine; during the third term, thirty-seven. Work done in immediate connection with class instruction from thirty to thirty-four hours per week, averaging grand total seventy hours, equally shared between two instructors.

CYRUS F. BRACKETT, M.D.,

Henry Professor of Physics.

———

I. My department is Physics, including
  (*a*) Elements of Mechanics.
  (*b*) Acoustics.
  (*c*) Heat.
  (*d*) Light.
  (*e*) Electricity.
  (*f*) Magnetism.

II. Four hours a week are given to the Juniors during the first session, and three during the second and third. I am occupied with the Seniors of the School of Science and the elective Seniors of the Academic course four hours a week throughout the year—the time being equally divided between the Scientific and Academic students.

III. With the Juniors, about one hour in four is occupied in recitation. The Seniors' work is of a different character and requires individual direction and instruction.

IV. Ganot's Physics is used as a text-book with the

39

Juniors. With the Seniors liberal and constant use is made of the literature of the subject, found in the College library, but no special text-book is used.

V. Two written examinations are required each year from the Juniors and a graduation thesis from the Seniors.

VI. Assistance is given in the laboratory during laboratory hours to such as apply for it.

VII. Laboratory work is required of the Seniors, in special courses, in Physics.

VIII. I would suggest that Physics be made an elective instead of a required study for the Seniors of the School of Science; in order that time need not be wasted by those unfit or not desiring to pursue the special work of the department;

And, secondly, that the Board of Trustees appoint a proper visiting committee of working physicists, who shall, at least once a session, examine the proficiency of the classes and the methods employed in the laboratory, and shall report in writing to the Board of Trustees, which would, it may be hoped, think best to publish the report. I should hope to see similar measures taken in every department of the College, as is done at some other institutions.

HENRY B. CORNWALL, A.M., E.M.,

Professor of Analytical Chemistry and Mineralogy.

I. Quantitative Chemical Analysis, for Seniors and Juniors, S. S., general and elective.

Qualitative Chemical Analysis, for Sophomores, S. S.

Laboratory Chemistry, illustrative of Theory and certain applications of Chemistry. Seniors, Academic, Elective.

Blowpipe Analysis, Freshmen, S. S.

Mineralogy, Sophomores, S. S., and Juniors, Elective, S. S.

Lithology, Seniors, S. S.

Assaying, dry method. Seniors, S. S. Elective.

II. Seniors, S. S. One hour a week.

Seniors, Academic Elect. Two hours in three weeks.

Juniors, S. S. One hour a week. This class is principally engaged in the Laboratory.

Sophomores, S. S. One hour in two weeks during First and Second Term; two hours a week in Third Term.

Freshmen, S. S. One hour a week during First Term; one hour in three weeks during Second and Third Terms.

This represents 4 1-10 hours of class-room work each week throughout the year.

III. Seniors and Juniors, three-fifths Lectures, two-fifths Recitations; Sophomores and Freshmen, one-half Lectures, one-half Recitations.

IV. Seniors and Juniors, S. S., Cairns's Analysis. Sophomores, S. S., Fresenius's Qual. Analysis. Freshmen, Dana's Manual of Mineralogy.

Senior Academic Elect. Cornwall's Laboratory Notes, printed exclusively for them.

The above books are indispensable.

V. Two-thirds of the recitations are written; all examinations are written, with addition of Laboratory Examinations for Sophomores and Freshmen, and practical examination in Mineralogy for Sophomores, S. S., and Juniors, S. S., Elective.

VI. Occasionally an hour a week to some special student or post-graduate, but otherwise only what is included under *VII.*

VII. I conduct the Laboratory work with the following classes in person:

Juniors—One hour a week.

Sophomores—Five hours weekly, except the time spent in the class-room.

Freshmen—One hour weekly during Second and Third Terms.

This represents 5 7-10 hours weekly throughout the year. The time is entirely taken up with the work, which requires my constant attention and is simply class-room work in another form, under my present system.

42

The Freshman class ought to have two hours weekly during Second and Third Terms, as they had when the school first started, and it is my intention to secure this as soon as the appointment of an Instructor in Drawing, now under consideration, makes it possible, by enabling us to re-arrange our schedule. My Laboratory hours will then represent 6 3-10 hours weekly.

No account is taken of the time spent in preparing lecture experiments.

VIII. It is very desirable to confine the work of Professors especially engaged with the School of Science classes as much as possible to work in the School of Science. The subject is one deserving the attention of the Trustees, since it can be, perhaps, remedied by transferring some of this work to any new appointees in Scientific branches.

I refer especially to work in Zoology, Biology, Mathematics and Modern Languages.

It is not in my Department, but it seriously affects it.

IX. Two short articles in the American Journal of Chemistry, giving the results of original work. I have on hand, awaiting a favorable opportunity for publication, the manuscript of a Manual of Blowpipe Analysis.

Note A. The above report takes no account of time spent in arranging and preparing collections of rocks and minerals for the Cabinet and the students' use, nor of time spent in analyzing and assaying the substances on which the students are to be engaged. The proper management of Chemical Laboratories involves the expenditure of time, not bearing at all upon class-room experiments, which may be estimated at one-third of the spare time of every working day.

Note B. Mr. Marsh has charge of the Quantitative Laboratory, the Assay Laboratory and the practical work of the Academic Elective Senior Class in Laboratory Chemistry, which occupies the whole time every day, except on Wednesday afternoons, when he will be employed in general work in the Department.

GEORGE MACLOSKIE, LL.D.,

Professor of Natural History.

I. Special topics taught by Professor.

(*a*) To School of Science classes—

    1. Structural Botany and classification of Plants.

    2. Microscopical Anatomy of Plants; their Physiology, Uses, Distribution; Practice of Examining Plants and of Herbarizing.

    3. General Zoology.

    4. Special course of Biology (including the Microscopical and Gross Anatomy of Animals, and Embryology.)

    5. Course of Human and Comparative Physiology.

    6. Course of Bible Instruction, viz. : Old Testament History of Redemption; Life of Jesus. These two subjects are taken on alternate years.

(*b*) To Academical Classes—

　　7. Outline course of Zoology.

　　8. Outline course of Botany.

　　9. Museum work: An Elective Class of Seniors (36 in it this year), taken through a series of practical examinations of vegetable and animal type-specimens.

II. Schedule of week's work:

Monday—3½–5 P. M., Biology. (Seniors, S. S., special class).

Tuesday—8½–10 A. M., Botany. (Freshman, S. S.) 10–12 A. M., Physiology. (Seniors, S. S.)

Wednesday—8½–10 A. M., Museum work. (Seniors, Academic). 3½–5 P. M., Museum work. (Seniors, Academic).

Thursday—9–10 A. M. and 11–12 A. M., 1st session, Biology. (Seniors, S. S., special class). 2d and 3d sessions, Botany and Zoology. (Sophomores, Academic.) 3½–5 P. M., Botany. (Sophomores, S. S.)

Friday—Occasional classes in first session. During second session, 9–11 A. M., Biology. (Seniors, S. S.)

Saturday—8.15 A. M., Conduct Chapel Exercises. 8.30 A. M., Bible Class. (Freshmen, S. S.) 9.00 A. M., Bible Class. (Sophomores, S. S.) 10.00 A. M., Zoology. (Juniors and Seniors, S. S.)

Total—An average of about 15 hours per week in actual instruction.

III. Proportion of hours given respectively to lectures and recitations:

1. As to Sophomore Class, (Academical).—Two recitations in the year are required of each student. The remainder of the time is devoted to Lectures.

2. As to the Senior Elective Class of Museum work and all the classes of the School of Science.—The time of each meeting is devoted in about equal proportions to recitations and to practical work under the direction of the Professor. His explanations sometimes take the form of short 'Lectures.'

IV. Text Books.

(a) Botany—Gray's "How Plants Grow," and "Manual of Botany;" Wood's "Fourteen Weeks in Botany;" McNab's "Morphology and Physiology;" Bessey's "Botany."

(b) Zoology—Tenney's (or Harbison's) outlines of Zoology; Packard's Zoology; Huxley's "Anatomy of Invertebrated Animals;" Huxley & Youmans' "Physiology and Hygiene;" Foster's "Physiology;" Huxley & Martin's "Biology."

V. Written Exercises.

1. With Academic Classes.—Written exercises are invited (though not required), from all students, and credit is given for such in returning grades. About half the students avail themselves of this arrangement, some of them giving many carefully prepared exercises.

2. As to School of Science Classes.—Frequent
exercises are required; say twenty in the
year from each Freshman and Sophomore,
including a botanical thesis from each
Sophomore, showing careful work with the
microscope. The Seniors are required to
prepare a graduation thesis on some subject
in Biology; and four or five exercises on
subjects studied are required during the
year from each student of the Junior and
Senior Class.

I'. Instruction out of recitation hours.

1. The students are all permitted and encour-
aged to do original work, examining specimens and preparing exercises and theses, in
the College rooms, using the apparatus belonging to the department, and having the
supervision and assistance of the Professor.
Many, both of the Scientific and of the
Academical students, make use of these
opportunities.

2. In springtime the classes studying Botany
are taken out by the Professor on Botanical
excursions, collecting and examining plants.

3. The character of this department is such that
the Professor must devote a considerable
portion of time before the meeting of each
class, to procuring specimens, and arranging
instruments, and after the meeting to placing
the instruments in their place of deposit,
and seeing that they are in proper condition.

VII. Laboratory work.

All the classes (excepting Sophomores, Academic) are continually exercised in Laboratory work. This consists in Analyzing, Classifying and Drying Plants, in studying their Histology by means of the Dissecting and Compound Microscopes, in describing the parts of plants; in dissecting and examining animals of different classes, hardening soft parts, making sections and preparing them for microscopic examination, and in studying their development from the egg.

VIII. Suggestions for Improvement.

Much is required before this department can occupy a satisfactory position in College.

1. An intelligent attendant is needed to save the Professor from searching out specimens (often taking journeys to the fields and rivers after them), to prepare apparatus and keep it in order, to clear away apparatus after it has been used, and to attend to our Botanical collections.

2. The supply of books for this department needs to be considerably increased. No satisfactory work can be done in Biology without access to a good library.

3. The books required for consultation ought to be removed to the same building with the Collections and Laboratories.

4. A seaside Laboratory for Summer work is required in connection with this department, to be located at Barnegat Inlet or some other convenient part of the coast.

5. A fellowship in Natural Science is needed to encourage and aid students who give promise of distinction in this work.

6. Some provision is needed in the College for instruction in drawing to the students who have to prepare illustrations for their exercises and theses in this department. [This is now supplied by a new Instructor in Graphics.]

IX. Publications by the Professor during the past year:

1. "The Proboscis of the Housefly." A paper read before the New Jersey Microscopical Society, and the New York Academy of Sciences. Published in American Naturalist, of March, 1880, with illustrations.

2. "The Endocranium and Maxillary Suspensorium of the Bee." A paper read before the American Association for Advancement of Science, (Boston, August, 1880); now in printer's hands for publication in the "Proceedings" of the Association, with six illustrations.

Also on subjects exterior to the Department he has edited the Journal of John Brainard, (formerly a Trustee of the College), and published other contributions.

50

JAMES O. MURRAY, D.D.,

Holmes Professor of Belles Lettres and English Language and Literature.

I. The English Language and Literature. The history of the English Language is taught in the Junior year, in connection with Lectures on Early English Literature. The course in English Literature, beginning with the Early English period, is continued to Wordsworth. Only representative authors are chosen from the vast field, and the aim of the course is to inspire a literary taste, and produce a literary culture by criticism of works, rather than by biographical details.

There is also a Post-Graduate class in this department pursuing the study of Early English and English Literature. This year I am meeting this class two hours a week.

Attached to this chair, is also a department of Biblical Instruction. For this purpose I meet the Junior class once a week. The Book studied is the Acts of the Apostles. Sometimes I have had a short course of lectures on the Prophets.

II. The hours employed in giving instruction are as follows: Senior class, one; Junior class, two; Post-Graduate class, two.

But in justice to myself I must ask attention to the amount of time consumed in reading and correcting essays (*vide* answer to Question *V.*)

III. Two lectures followed by a recitation.

IV. Lounsbury's History of the English Language.

V. Senior Class—

    1st Term, 1 Essay, 10 pages.
       "   1 Chapel Stage Oration.
    2d Term, 1 Essay, 12 pages.
       "   1 Commencement Speech.

Junior Class—

    1st Term, 2 Essays, 6 pages.
       "   1 Speech.
    2d Term, 2 Essays.
    3d Term, 1 Essay, 8 pages.

As the classes average about one hundred men, I have from the Junior class 3,200 MSS. pages; from the Senior class, 2,200; total, 5,400 of essays alone. Last year Prof. Raymond had the speeches under his care.

VI. I have been accustomed to meet the Senior class for readings in English Literature once a fortnight during the winter months. If time and strength permit, I would like to do the same with the Juniors. No work does more for this department, than work of this sort.

VII. There are two suggestions as to improvement of this department:

1. The elocutionary instruction should be put at once upon a different basis. [The recent appointment of Prof. Raymond to the Chair of Oratory fully meets this suggestion.]

2. The study of Early English should be made optional in the Senior year.

CHARLES McMILLAN, C.E.,

Professor of Civil Engineering and Applied Mathematics.

I. In the Freshman Class (C. E. and B. S.)

1st. *Elements of Industrial Drawing.* Beginning with instructions as to the use of drawing instruments and materials, and the proper mode of handling and adjusting them, the student is drilled in the execution of different kinds of lines; of right, curved and broken line shading; and in the use of brushes and colors in tinting, wet and dry shading and stippling. After acquiring a certain degree of skill in the preceding, the student is exercised in the modes of representing different materials both by conventional symbols and by imitating scenic effects. This course is followed by

2d. *Elementary Projections.* This is given by lectures and drawing exercises, and is designed to expand the application of the preceding course to elementary drawing in three dimensions and to break ground for the succeeding course in Descriptive Geometry. The drawing is almost entirely from models.

3d. *Geodesy.* The fair days of Autumn and Spring are devoted to the field work of chain surveying and compass surveying. This is preceded by a very short

53

course of lectures, barely sufficient to cover the necessary instruction as to the manipulation of instruments.

The theory and principles are afterwards thoroughly unfolded by recitations from text-books, with supplementary notes. (Course given to C. E.'s only.)

In the Sophomore Class (C. E. and B. S.)

1st. *Descriptive Geometry, Shades and Shadows and Perspective.* This course, like the first and second of the Freshman year, although not properly belonging to a chair of Civil Engineering, is given, for want of a better arrangement, by my assistant under my direction. The general students in the School of Science take the same course as the engineering students, with the exception of warped surfaces and some special problems.

2d. *Topographical Drawing* (given to C. E.'s only), consisting of drawing exercises in the elements of pen topography, and ending with the execution of a finished pen and ink map of the compass survey made at the close of the Freshman year.

3d. *Geodesy* (given to C. E.'s only). The course consists mainly of field work in the adjustment of instruments, leveling, contouring and plane triangulation. It is preceded by about a dozen very exacting recitations on the theory of the above operations.

In the Junior Class (C. E. and B. S.)

1st. *Topographical Drawing* (given to C. E.'s only), consisting of the execution of plates in colored topography, and closing with a study in landscape design; also, of the construction of hydrographic charts, plans of town and mine surveys.

2d. *Machine Drawing and Stereotomy* (given to C. E.'s only), consisting of graphic solutions of problems in cinematics, laying out tooth curves and of the general study of trochoidal curves; also of the preparation of working drawings of details of structures, and of a finished drawing from measurement of some structure, or piece of mechanism.

3d. *Geodesy* (given to C. E.'s only), consisting of recitations and field work in town, mine and plane table surveys, and in hydrography.

4th. *Rational Mechanics.* This subject is taught to candidates for both degrees with the exception of those students who elect Natural History or Chemistry. The instruction is given, as far as possible, with the aid of the calculus, and presupposes that the students have an intimate knowledge of mathematics. An endeavor is made to reach the standard attained in the same subject in the Military Academy and in the Rensselaer Institute at Troy, N. Y.

IN THE SENIOR CLASS. (C. E.)

1st. *Physical and Experimental Mechanics.* This consists of two courses, both from text-book ; the one on elasticity and strength of materials, and the other on practical hydraulics. Both courses are coupled with illustration and experiment.

2d. *The Theory of Motors.* This course covers the general theory of water wheels, water pressure engines and steam engines. It is given from text-book, with illustrations.

3d. *Stability of Structures*, or the theory of framed structures; *i. e.,* of roofs and bridges ; and of block structures; as walls, arches, &c. The first is taught from text-book, the second from lectures.

4th. *Constructions*. A descriptive course taken from Wheeler's text-book, with notes, ending with lectures on the design and construction of water works, sewerage, roads, railways and tunnels.

5th. *Geodesy*, consisting of lectures on road surveying followed by field practice in reconnoitering, locating and cross-sectioning. This is followed by a short course of lectures on Higher Geodesy.

6th. *Stereotomy*, consisting of a course on stone cutting—taken from text-book. It is coupled with exercises in the laying out of stone mason's templates and patterns. One set of these is usually tested by applying them to the cutting of a "stone" from a rough block of plaster with the aid of the square, straight edge, and other mason's implements.

7th. *Topographical Drawing*, consisting of the preparation of a colored map of the railway survey with finished drawings of proposed profile and sections.

8th. *Graduating Thesis*. In this the student receives general instructions as to the treatment of the subject—its arrangement and illustration. The main work of the Professor, however, is in keeping up a running check on all the computations in order to avoid the use of wrong formulæ, to detect erroneous computations, and to prevent unjust conclusions.

As the student's traditions in regard to professional theses become more settled, and attain a better form, with age, the severity of this labor on the part of the instructor will become less, and the graduating theses will approach, in point of originality and thoroughness, more nearly what they should be.

II. The instruction in the preceding subjects is given with the aid of one assistant. How much time is devoted thereto by each one of us is a difficult question to answer conscientiously, because the unavoidable clashing of hours in the schedule makes a confusion in our work which prevents the laying out of studies for any considerable period ahead. Also, because I have pursued the policy, not only of directing the work of my assistant, but likewise of taking part in the exercises often enough to keep up a fair acquaintance with the progress of his classes. This participation in my assistant's work has hitherto occurred about twice a week during recitations, and much oftener in the practical exercises, especially in drawing.

It may be fairly said that in the first term I have conducted thirteen of the regular exercises allotted to my department, while my assistant has had charge of fourteen. The equivalents in hours would be twenty-two and twenty-five and a half hours respectively.

During five weeks of the second term, twenty-nine exercises per week are required of us, of which I have endeavored to give fifteen and my assistant fourteen, equivalent to twenty and thirty hours per week respectively.

In the latter part of the second term the schedule requires twenty-five exercises, of which I take twelve and my assistant thirteen, devoting thereto twenty-one and twenty-five hours.

In the third term this continues with the addition of thesis work, which, alone, if properly superintended,

57

requires an amount of time equivalent to about one-half of the entire third term. I have not included in the above the time spent with special students, especially with those who purpose ultimately taking the degree of C. E., nor that devoted by me to the weekly testing of my Assistant's classes and to the direction of his practical exercises, nor that necessarily consumed in the care of apparatus and in the preparation and assembling of the same for illustrating lectures, or the text-book. I have also left out of the above estimate the time which both my assistant and I have given to students who have asked permission to continue their work after hours; that is to say, between exercises, after twelve, and occasionally, in field work, after the evening Chapel hour. Whenever possible, we have continued their exercises, but with the distinct understanding that they must not infringe on the claims of other departments. The extra time thus given in Spring and Autumn has amounted to from 15 to 20 per cent. of the schedule time. In Winter about 10 per cent. will fairly represent it.

III. The bulk of the work is done with the aid of text-books. Lectures are mainly auxiliaries, *i. e.*, they either initiate, explain, or add to, the matter of the text-book. There are three exceptions, viz., the lectures on Stability of Structures; Water Works and Sewerage; Roads, Railways and Tunnels.

It will be safe to say that only about one-sixth of all the recitations are from lectures.

IV. Gillespie's Land Surveying.
Gillespie's Higher Surveying.
Warren's Elements of Descriptive Geometry.

Warren's Stone Cutting.
Smith's Mechanics.
Wood's Mechanics (on trial).
Wood's Strength of Materials.
Burr's Stresses in Roofs and Bridges.
Eddy's Thermodynamics.
Wheeler's Elements of Civil Engineering.
Bresse's Hydraulic Motors.
Searles's Field Book for Engineers.

V. The black-board exercises of my recitations may be justly regarded as written exercises in purpose and effect. Four-fifths of my recitations, on an average, require black-board exercises; the total being ten or twelve black-board exercises per week for the entire department.

At least one written examination in the department is required every year by the rules of the College.

With the exception of these, I have no written exercises other than the graduating thesis. This paper, when properly prepared, consumes an amount of time on the part of the student, equivalent to from three to four weeks of whole days. I have occasionally known it to require more time.

The subject is generally selected, and the drawings begun in the first term of the Senior year. The students devote to this work such time as they can spare throughout the rest of the year, and, with the exception of two or three days' rest after the final examinations, the whole of the senior vacation preceding commencement.

VI. My exercises consist of—
1st. Lectures.
2d. Recitations on lectures and from text-book.

3d. Drawing exercises, including sketching to scale and laying out measurements from models; also mapping from actual surveys.

4th. Field work in surveying, locating and staking out.

5th. Laboratory work in testing materials in hydraulic experiments, in erection of structures, and in the experimental determination of power and efficiency of steam and hydraulic motors.

6th. Thesis work.

VII. This question is answered in the fifth section of the reply to the sixth question. Sections three and four of the same reply may be adverted to as possibly coming within the scope of this question. They refer to practical exercises, the main purpose of which is to make the students skillful manipulators.

VIII. The first suggestion which I would take the liberty of making is, that all the instruction in instrumental and free-hand drawing, excepting topographical drawing, be gathered into a complete department, and that a competent instructor be placed in charge of it. I would beg leave to suggest that this department be designated either as the Department of Graphics, or as that of Descriptive Geometry, Stereotomy and Free-Hand Drawing—the latter indicating the sub-divisions. [An Instructor in the department of Graphics has just been appointed.]

Another suggestion which I would beg leave to make is, that the standard of requirements for the translation of students from class to class be raised by establishing some grade, higher than 50, say 60, to begin with, as the minimum grade or number on which a student may be declared passed. I believe that a good standard cannot be reached in a scientific, or a professional school with a minimum limit of 50. It should be at least 60. In this connection it may be well to allude to the tact, that the theoretical and actual meanings of any such minimum limit are somewhat different; the latter being always lower than the former by an appreciable amount. I would state also that my department would be benefited by gradually raising the standard for admission in Mathematics so as to include the whole of Plane Geometry, and Algebra through Quadratics.

I would further suggest that a sharper tracing by the Trustees of the lines of separation between interlocking subjects of different professors, followed by a recasting of the schedule with especial reference to the natural and logical sequence of the studies, might result in a decided gain of time, by avoiding a repetition of the same subject in different courses. I incline to the opinion that some changes in these particulars made with care, and judiciously, would be of advantage to all the courses of the School of Science.

I would beg leave to suggest, finally, that a small visiting committee of educated civil engineers of the standing of Gen. McClellan, Mr. A. J. Cassatt, or Mr. A. L. Holley, might be of great help to the Department of Civil Engineering by attending its examinations, giving it the benefit of their advice or suggestions, and reporting its condition and progress to the Board of Trustees.

IX. I have published nothing during the past year.

CHARLES A. YOUNG, Ph.D., LL.D.,

Professor of Astronomy.

I. (*a*) General Astronomy to the whole Senior Class —both Academic and Scientific.

(*b*) Practical Astronomy—elective to members of the Academic Senior Class; required of the Civil Engineers.

II. About eight; but the number varies. During the first term I have the class in General Astronomy twice a week; generally in two divisions, making four hours. The class in Practical Astronomy *recites* once a week, and if the weather is fair I am generally occupied with them three or four hours during the evenings of the week. During the second and third term I have the General Astronomy only once a week.

III. I intend to give about one lecture to two recitations.

IV. I use Newcomb & Holden's Astronomy for the General Class, and Loomis's Practical Astronomy for the Elective Class.

V. A written recitation about the middle of each term for the General Class, besides the regular examination. Last term, however, the written recitation was omitted on account of special circumstances. The work of the Practical Astronomy Class is nearly all in writing.

VI. The General Class visit the Observatory to look at various astronomical objects three or four times each term.

(I am not quite sure as to the meaning of the question). I have had during last year three pupils in Astronomy, not belonging to College Classes. One— A. S. Flint—has been appointed Assistant to Dr. Gould at the National Observatory of the Argentine Republic at Cordova, South America.

VII. Nearly the whole work of the Practical Astronomy Class is of the nature of Laboratory work, consisting in the making of Astronomical observations and their reduction.

VIII. It is very unfortunate that the General Astronomy does not come until Senior year. The consequence is, that although the College has decidedly the best outfit in the country for Astronomical instruction, the number that take practical Astronomy as an elective is very small. The general course ought to precede the special.

Another objectionable feature is the manner in which the exercises are arranged—one or two a week, instead of being brought together, one a day or so, until the subject is finished. If this scattering of the exercises can be remedied and the subject of General Astronomy thrown into Junior year, a great gain would be made.

IX. November, 1879—Papers read (not published) before National Academy of Sciences on (*a*) (1) Color Correction of Gaussian Object Glass.

(*b*) (2) Duplicity of Lockyer's Basic Lines.

(*c*) 'Nature,' November, 1879—Re-reversal of Sodium Lines.

(*d*) 'The Observatory,' November, 1879—Observations of the Satellites of Mars.

(*e*) 'The Observatory,' November, 1879—Note of the *b* Lines in the Solar Spectrum.

(*f*) Princeton Review, January, 1880—Recent progress in Solar Astronomy.

(*g*) American Journal Science and Art, March—Measures of the Polar and Equatorial Diameters of Mars. (Mr. McNeill assisted in the preparation of this paper).

(*h*) A. A. A. S. Proceedings, 1879—A method of investigating the errors of the pivots of Meridian Instrument.

(*i*) Astronomische Nachrichten, June, 1880—Observations on Comet *b* 1880. (Reductions by Mr. McNeill).

(*k*) American Journal Science, June—The Color Correction of certain Achromatic Object Glasses.

(*l*) American Journal Science, June—Experiments upon Edison's Dynamo Electric Machines and Lamp. (In connection with Prof. Brackett).

(*m & n*) Papers before A. A. A. S. at Boston, August, 1880 (not yet published).

1. Spectroscopic notes on observations since June, 1879.

2. Note on the Thermo-Electric Electro-Motive Power of Iron and Platinum, with reference to Exner's recent experiments.

Besides these I have published a few short articles on scientific matters as Editorials in the N. Y. Times, and have furnished the Physical and Astronomical Notes for The Independent.

A good deal of time has been spent also in the reduction of the observations for determining the latitude and longitude of our Observatory, which will soon be published.

I have in hand at present an article on the 'Solar Heat' for the Popular Science Monthly, and a book (nearly finished) on the Sun, for Appleton's International Series.

REV. S. STANHOPE ORRIS, Ph.D.,

Ewing Professor of Greek Language and Literature.

I. The Greek Language and Literature; the Doctrine of the Formation of Words in Greek; the Principles of Greek Etymology; Greek Prose Composition; the Theories of the Origin of Language; the Causes underlying and determining Dialectic Varieties; the Philosophy of Plato; Exegesis of the Gospel of John in Greek.

II. Thirteen hours in class-room.

III. Five-sixths to recitations, and one-sixth to dictations and lectures.

IV. My classes read Herodotus, Theocritus, Cebes and Lucian; Demosthenes—The Philippics and the Oration on the Crown; Plato—The Phædo, Gorgias, Protagoras, Phædrus, Theætetus and Republic; Æschylus—The Agamemnon and the Prometheus Bound.

V. On the subjects in which I give instruction, I require from the Sophomores and Juniors each, three written exercises during the year; from the Seniors two, and from the Freshmen one. The Greek Prose is both a written and an oral exercise, constituting part of

66

almost every recitation, especially in the Sophomore year.

VI. I give instruction to a post-graduate class in the Philosophy of Plato in connection with his Republic.

VII. I have had and hope still to have optional readings with members of my classes.

VIII. In accordance with our schedule of studies as at present arranged, the Freshmen recite every week in three different Greek authors to as many different instructors. The result is, that their interest in no one author is as controlling as it might otherwise be, and those of us who meet them but once a week, labor to great disadvantage. The interests of this class, in the Greek department, would be promoted by greater concentration of labor on their part and ours.

IX. I am writing on all the subjects on which I give instruction, and on one or two of these I may in course of time publish the results of my studies.

CHARLES G. ROCKWOOD, Jr., Ph.D.,

Professor of Mathematics.

I. I am giving instruction as follows:

'To the Academic Department. Freshman Class. Algebra—One hour per week to each student through the year, as per vote of the Trustees in June, 1877.

To the School of Science. Freshman Class. Algebra --Five hours per week during first term. Geometry— Five hours per week during second and part of third term. Plane Trigonometry—Five hours per week during part of third term.

Sophomore Class. Spherical Trigonometry and Analytical Geometry—Four hours per week during second and third terms.

Junior Class. Calculus—Five hours per week during first term.

II. During the first term, fourteen hours per week as follows: Freshman Class, Academic (four divisions), four hours; Freshman Class, School of Science, five hours; Junior Class, School of Science, five hours; total, fourteen hours.

During the second and third terms, thirteen hours per week as follows: Freshman Class, Academic (four

68

divisions), four hours; Freshman Class, School of Science, five hours; Sophomore Class, School of Science, four hours; total, thirteen hours.

III. My exercises are almost entirely recitations in form; but every one contains more or less oral instruction not in the text-book, which might I suppose fairly be called "lecturing," and sometimes the whole hour is devoted to such work. Occasionally more formal lectures are given.

IV. The text-books used are as follows:

School of Science, Freshman Class—Well's University Algebra; Chauvenet's Geometry; Olney's Trigonometry.

Sophomore Class—Olney's Trigonometry; Loomis' Analytical Geometry.

Junior Class—Loomis' Differential and Integral Calculus.

Academic Department, Freshman Class—Ray's Algebra (at present, but with intention to change).

V. Written exercises to be prepared at home are rarely required, if ever. Written work on the blackboard forms an important part of every recitation.

VI. Not regularly. I am always ready to give assistance outside of the class hour, and the students are in the habit of availing themselves of this privilege almost every day. I have no pupils outside of the College.

VII. My department does not call for any exercise similar to laboratory work.

VIII. I would respectfully suggest, as a matter which in my judgment calls for immediate attention, that some change be made which will permit the instruction in

69

Algebra to the Freshman Class of the Academic Department to be consolidated into one term instead of being, as now, spread through the entire year with recitations once a week. I am not able to suggest, however, any detailed plan of adjustment which does not involve considerable changes. My opinion is that it would be wise to abandon the present arrangement, even if the alternative should be to recommit the instruction in Algebra to the hands of a tutor. I do not undervalue the advantage of having parts of the Mathematical instruction of Freshman year in charge of a Professor, but I think it can easily be shown that the disadvantages of the present plan decidedly overbalance any advantage from that cause.

I would also suggest that in my opinion it is very desirable, at an early day, to increase the Mathematical requirements for entrance to the School of Science, and I am prepared at an appropriate time to make a definite proposal looking in that direction, and to give my reasons therefor.

LX. Article in American Journal of Science and Arts. Vol. xix., pp. 295–9. April, 1880. Title, "Notices of Recent American Earthquakes, No. 9."

Numerous Brief Memoranda in same Journal as below.

Vol. xviii., pp. 159, 228, 308.
Vol. xix., pp. 162, 163, 334, 334, 426, 427, 496.
Vol. xx., p. 159.

REV. THEODORE W. HUNT, Ph.D.,

Professor of Rhetoric and English Language.

I. Anglo-Saxon and Modern English Art of Discourse. Bible (temporarily assigned).

II. Regular Teaching, eight hours; Optional and Post-Graduate, two hours; Essay Criticism, two hours; total, twelve hours.

III. Recitations and Lectures consume, respectively, two-thirds and one-third of the time.

IV. March's Anglo-Saxon Grammar and Reader; Study of Words, (Trench); Rhetoric, (Hart); Outline of Notes, (Hunt).

V. Written Exercises are, of course, an essential part of my work. They vary from five to seven a year for each class, (Freshman and Sophomore).

VI. In the line of essay criticism I give assistance (to students), outside of the regular course.

VII. The critical work of the English Department is my only laboratory work.

VIII. (*a*) More attention to the study of the English Language. An entire year could well be devoted to this work.

71

(*b*) The Philosophic Study of Discourse and
the Art of Criticism as Elective in the
higher classes. This is an imperative
need.

(*c*) Help in some form as to the instruction of
the Freshman Class and the work of
Essay Criticism. The demands of the
department in the line of independent
research call urgently for this.

IX. During the year, I have prepared several articles, two of which are now in the hands of the printer.

I have, moreover, written extra courses of lectures—philological and literary—rather for the possible needs of the class-room than for publication.

I am also preparing a work—The Principles of Discourse—which I hope to publish. It presents the subject from the mental standpoint, and is designed for use in the upper classes of our American Colleges. To such original work as this I am devoted, and am urgent in asking some relief in elementary work and essay criticism so that I may be of service to the cause of English in this direction.

As to English Literature, Dr. Murray will speak.

I may suggest, however, that an Elective in that study is a present need.

Vocal Drill of some kind could be given with profit to most of our students.

WILLIAM M. SLOANE, Ph.D.,

Adjunct Professor of Latin.

It has been my duty to instruct the Freshman Class in Latin Prose Composition and the Sophomore Class in Latin Prose Composition and Terence. The instruction in the Freshman Class is conducted with a view to familiarizing the students with the grammar and idioms of the Latin language. To this end the following plan is pursued: An exercise prepared for the purpose is dictated on one day; the student prepares a written translation and gives it to me on the second day, and on the third day the class recites on it, turning the English into Latin, in my presence, as they would turn a Latin text into English. This occupies half of each hour; the other half hour is devoted to the explanation of minor peculiarities in the use of Latin words which an ordinary school grammar would leave unnoticed. The instruction is conveyed by dictating the principle, by adducing examples and by a constant interchange of question and answer with the students, who translate these examples at sight, either from English into Latin or from Latin into English, as the case may be, and thus have as much practice in acquiring familiarity with the forms and meanings of words

73

as the time allows. I have at irregular intervals
during the year three or four written recitations of
an hour each, which are not announced before hand,
and these exercises being in the nature of a review, are
intended to keep constantly fresh in each student's
mind the results of his work up to that time.

During the Sophomore Year I continue the above-
mentioned course on a higher and more difficult plane.
The exercises required to be translated into Latin are
idiomatic English, being taken from histories or
speeches, and the impossibility of translating them
literally is intended to give to the students some acquaintance with Latin style. The additional instruction is therefore more especially devoted to the
rhetorical expression of the Romans, their choice and
arrangement of words and the distinguishing characteristics of their diction. Each division of the Sophomore
Class also reads a play of Terence with me during the
year. Attention is directed to the Archaisms of
Terence in orthography, grammar and style, to the
influence of Greek literature upon Roman letters, to
the introduction of Greek metres into Latin and their
application as showing the probable colloquial pronunciation of Latin, to the life and morals of the
Romans as illustrated by their comedy, and to the
general literary quality of Terence's writings. The
class reviews in each recitation the preceding lesson,
and at the close of the term again reviews the whole
play ; it reads during the year about fifteen pages at
sight, and has several written recitations of the same
character as those which are required of the Freshman
Class. In addition the class is required to prepare one

74

essay each year on some given subject connected with the author. The last subjects were Terence and Plautus compared, and Roman Comedy. The class reads with me during the third term, the Germania or Agricola of Tacitus.

In the past I have been employed four hours a week in instructing the Freshman Class, and the same number in instructing the Sophomore Class. The change made in my position will give me further employment during fourteen weeks in instructing the Junior Class two hours a week.

The only text-book which I use is Fleckeisen's text of Terence, but the Latin Department requires that every student shall possess or have access to a Grammar, Dictionary, Dictionary of Antiquities and Biography, and some good Roman History. At the beginning of each term I name to the class the best books of reference on the subject with which they are to be occupied.

The Freshman and Sophomore Classes have each a weekly written exercise in Latin Prose Composition and about four written recitations a year. The Sophomore Class is required to write one essay a year.

During two years I have been occupied two hours a week in instructing in German and reading Kant in the original with graduate students. The number in different years has varied, two being the lowest and nine the highest.

SAMUEL R. WINANS, A. B.,
Ex-FELLOW OF PRINCETON COLLEGE,

Tutor in Greek.

I. Greek. Prominence given to elementary drilling, review of Greek Grammar, with elucidation of principles both in Forms and in Syntax; instruction in Greek Composition; translating Greek, with whatever of history, literary discussion, &c., is incidental to the author read.

II. Twelve hours,—arranged as in schedule printed in the Catalogue; q. v.,—*Greek Prose and Memorabilia.*

III. Recitations almost exclusively; very rarely in the year a whole hour may be given to lecture or talk.

IV. Goodwin's Greek Grammar, 2d ed.; Goodwin's Moods and Tenses; Jones' Greek Prose Composition; Sidgwick's advanced ditto; Xenophon's Memorabilia; and toward the end of the year some second text, as Xenophon's Symposium, or Aristophanes' Clouds, &c.

V. Translations from English into Greek: a set of exercises from text-book, and original,—one each week during the greater part of the year (25–30).

A classical essay was assigned this department last

76

year, to be of 4 pp. The subjects for the past year—all related directly to our studies—were : (1) Xenophon as Socrates' Biographer ; (2) Socrates' Domestic Relations ; (3) The Socrates of Aristophanes ; (4) The Influence of the Clouds against Socrates ; (5) Socrates before the Court; (6) The Mission of Socrates ; (7) What was τὸ δαιμόνιον? (8) Socrates for the Divine Existence ; (9) Did Socrates really introduce " new divinities ;" (10) Socrates' Theory of Virtue ; (11) The Allegory of Hercules at the Road-forks ; (12) Metrical Version of Cleanthes' Hymn to Zeus.

Written examinations in October, December and June ; oral in April.

VI. Year before last I conducted during the Winter an optional class in reading Greek Comedy. A dozen of my pupils of the year previous joined it : genuine enthusiasm was developed, and the course was profitable. Was too busy to do this last year, though solicited to renew the course ; expect to form such a class this Winter.

VII. A course of reading is suggested.

VIII. Yes : (1) The desirability of some arrangement by which the Freshmen can be pursuing fewer studies in the department at the same time. The only thing in favor of the present plan originally was that it distributed evenly and simply the work of the various instructors. The disadvantage to the student is obvious enough.

(2) The immediate addition of one book of Anabasis to the entrance requirement; another book (of Homer) possibly to follow in a few years. Candidates put too

77

little time on the Greek to secure a right preparation, *i. e.*, a reasonably fair quality.

IX. "Xenophon's Memorabilia of Socrates," with Introduction and Notes. 16mo., pp. xxiv. + 265. Already reported as adopted and in use at a score of colleges.

GEORGE BRUCE HALSTED, A.M., Ph.D.,

Ex-FELLOW OF PRINCETON COLLEGE. AND OF JOHNS
HOPKINS UNIVERSITY.

Tutor in Mathematics.

I. To the undergraduates I teach Geometry, Mensuration and the History of Mathematics.

In addition to this, I give Post-Graduate courses in the pure sciences, mathematics and symbolic logic. Last year I gave a course on the Philosophy and Methods of the Calculus, and instruction in Modern Analytics. This year I give courses on Determinants, Quaternions, Projective Geometry, Modern Higher Algebras and Logics.

II. I teach thirteen hours a week.

III. I give always more than half these hours to recitations.

IV. I use as text-books Todhunter's Euclid and Halsted's Treatise on Mensuration, also Tait's Quaternions and Scott's Determinants.

V. I have required the original investigation and treatment of special topics assigned by me in connection with class work. Some of these written exercises have been from sixteen to twenty pages of legal cap in length.

VI. Besides my regular Undergraduate and Post-Graduate courses, I have taught a class made up of the best Undergraduate Mathematicians who met at my room for help and deeper work on the subjects taught to the upper classes in College.

VII. I give my Undergraduate Class an exceedingly large number of practical exercises in Geometry and Mensuration, many of them entirely original.

VIII. I do not ask any change in my work or my salary, but simply a change of title.

IX. 1. Modern Mathematicians as Educators. Nassau Literary Magazine, November, 1876.

2. Is Formal Logic a Branch of Mathematics? Nassau Literary Magazine, February, 1877.

3. On Spencer's Classification of the Abstract Sciences. Popular Science Monthly, 1877.

4. The New Ideas about Space. Popular Science Monthly, 1877.

5. Bibliography of Hyper-Space and Non-Euclidean Geometry. Three articles in the American Journal of Mathematics, during 1878 and 1879.

6. History of Exact Rectilinear Motion. Van Nostrand's Engineering Magazine, 1878.

7. Mechanical Conversion of Motion. Van Nostrand's Engineering Magazine, 1878; reprinted by "World of Science," London.

8. On Jevon's Criticism of Boole's Logic. English Philosophical Magazine "Mind," 1878.

9. Boole's Logical Method. Journal of Speculative Philosophy, 1878.
10. Statement and Reduction of Syllogism. Journal of Speculative Philosophy, 1878.
11. Algorithmic Division in Logic. Journal of Speculative Philosophy, 1879.
12. Basis for a Dual Logic. Thesis for the degree of Doctor of Philosophy at Johns Hopkins University.
13. On the First English Euclid. American Journal of Mathematics, 1879.
14. Algebras, Spaces, Logics. In Popular Science Monthly for August, 1880.
15. During much of the past year I have been working hard on a Mathematical Treatise, published by the firm of Ginn & Heath, of Boston. This is a treatment entirely distinct from anything existing in the English language, of the whole subject of Metrical Geometry, and will, I think, especially mark an epoch in Stereometry.

I have already in MS. a History of Mathematics; an Edition of Euclid from Modern Standpoints; and a Treatise on Dual Logic.

81

CHARLES R. WILLIAMS, A.M.,

Ex-FELLOW OF PRINCETON COLLEGE.

I. My department is Latin with the Freshman Class. The special topics are as follows: In the first and second terms I read portions of the history of Livy, from the I, the XXI, and the XXII books. This year I have begun with the XXI. In the third term it has been usual to read some portion of Cicero's minor philosophical works, as a book of the Tusculan Disputations, or *De Amicitia*, or *De Senectute*. Besides this a careful review of Latin Grammar is undertaken, and regular lessons are assigned. Moreover the study of early Roman history is pursued.

II. I teach twelve hours a week. Three hours with each of the four divisions of the Freshmen.

III. Recitations are the rule, lectures the rare exception.

IV. Text-books are made use of. For Livy and Cicero, various editions; but Chase and Stuart's are recommended and most used. Allen and Greenough's Latin Grammar is employed for class-room work. For Roman history, last year Ihne's Early Rome, supplemented by lectures, was used. The current year Leighton's History of Rome will take its place.

I‴. Once or twice each term written recitations will be required. A portion of the text will be assigned for translation, and questions asked thereupon.

VI. I have in a few instances given instruction in preparatory studies to private pupils.

VII. I have no laboratory work and nothing corresponding to it.

VIII. The Freshman course in Latin, I think, would be materially improved if the work of the students were limited to fewer subjects under fewer different instructors. During the greater part of last year the Freshmen recited every week to three different instructors upon four different subjects. Horace once, Latin prose once, Roman history once, Livy twice. I am persuaded that students, so early in their course at any rate, can not at one time pursue so many studies to the best advantage.

IX. No.

HERMANN HUSS, Ph.D.,

Assistant Professor in Modern Languages.

I. To answer this question satisfactorily, the Instructor having been connected with the College but a short time, hopes to be excused, if, instead of saying what he is teaching, he states what he proposes to teach.

.(A.)—IN THE JOHN C. GREEN SCHOOL OF SCIENCE.

1. In the Freshman year a rapid course is taken through the whole grammar of the German and French languages, with the view of making the beginner at first acquainted with nothing but its most important points, all details which would only bewilder his mind being carefully excluded. To impress these salient points on the student's mind, the greatest stress is laid upon his memorizing good prose carefully selected and progressively arranged by the instructor for this purpose. Concrete examples offer a far better hold to memory, and keep up a livelier interest than dry abstract rules, and the knowledge of the example necessarily involves the knowledge of the rule illustrated by it.

It is by this method that everything is avoided that

84

is tedious to the beginner. For not only the memorizing of dry rules, but—what is even a greater task—the committing of vocabularies is spared to him. To be sure, he has to commit the words of his prose-models to memory, but there is a great difference in committing isolated words as presented in a vocabulary, and words connected in sentences, the former being dead and silent mechanisms, the latter living, speaking organisms appearing in their individual color, expression, light and shade.

Thus, at the end of the first year the student has formed his pronunciation, is well posted in the leading grammatical rules, and provided with a considerable stock of words.

2. In the Sophomore year a second and much briefer course through the grammar is requisite to make up what has been passed over in the first; at the same time a reader is used, and particular attention paid to the study of the intricate German construction. There cannot too much stress be laid upon this important point, for it is one of the strongest convictions of the writer that the German language, with the great difficulty of its construction, has to fulfil, if no other, a far reaching educational *mission* at the School of Science in general. All that is claimed for the classical languages concerning the formal culture of mind can be claimed for the German language. For German, as Latin and Greek, forms its long periods exclusively under the precepts of logic; hence it is only under the guidance of strict logic that the foreigner can construe a German period, and extricate himself from its labyrinth. What can there be devised more salutary for the formal culture of the

student's mind? How can his intellect be better trained and his logical powers better drilled?

3. In the Junior year. Having during the two previous years fully mastered all the technicalities of the language, the class is now initiated into the literature of French and German. The choicest pieces of Goethe, Schiller, Lessing, Racine, Corneille, Molière, are read and commented on. Still, merely grammatical comments, because so apt to stifle the student's interest, and to spoil his enjoyment of the artistic beauties of the author, are only touched upon, when unavoidable, in order to keep his attention free and open for their more important ethical and æsthetic teachings.

To keep up, however, the practice in grammar, a separate hour is given to translations from English into German and French. These useful exercises may be commenced in the preceding year, if time and circumstances favor.

4. In the Senior year the literary studies are continued, but theory claims a place by the side of practice—that is, lectures are delivered on the history of the French and German languages; on their relation to other languages of the Indo-German stock; on the various stages they went through before assuming their present form; on their principal literary monuments; on the style and tendency of their great writers as well as on the religious, moral, social and political influence they exercised on their nation in special and on mankind in general.

At the same time a strictly *scientific* reader is used in the class in order to fit the student for reading with facility the standard works of his future profession.

In the Senior Class, or if circumstances are favorable, as early as in the Junior Class, the instructor uses the foreign tongues as a vehicle of communication, and insists upon the students doing the same. Also compositions in French and German, as well as translating German and French prose at sight, will be expected from him.

(B)—Academic Department.

Here the instructor's aim is a lower one on account of the exceedingly limited time allotted to his department, but his method is, on the whole, the same. As to the topics taught, the scientific reader used in the School of Science is excluded; in compensation the academic student being familiar with Latin, is in his French studies made acquainted with the results of comparative philology.

II. In the first and second terms :

(*a*) In the class-room. -   -   -   14½
(*b*) In looking over written exercises, -   10

Total, -   - ·   -   -   24½

In the third term :

(*a*) In the class-room,   -   -   -   18½
(*b*) In looking over written exercises, -   15

Total, -   -   -   -   33½

III. Not having charge of the Seniors at present, the work of the Instructor consists exclusively in recitations.

IV. In French : Keetel's Collegiate Course ; Lacombe's " Petite Histoire de France;" later, Prof. Kargé's Scientific Reader, now in preparation.

87

In German : Otto's Grammar ; Whitney's Reader ; Hodge's Scientific Reader.

V. Written exercises are in the two lower classes required every week without exception, to recapitulate all that has been taught during the week. The exercises are taken home by the instructor, and the errors underscored, the correction being required from the student himself. When they are handed in for the second time, the instructor looks them over once more, to make sure if the corrections have been properly attended to.

VI. Since quite a number of students recently joined the Sophomore Class without having ever studied French, it was necessary to bring them up to the standard of the class. Consequently the instructor meets them twice a week for oral and written exercises.

VII. No.

VIII. No.

IX. Since my last publication, "German as pronounced in Hanover," Hahn, Hanover, 1879, I I have been giving all my time to the preparation of a German text-book on the principles pointed out above.

S. G. PEABODY,

Associate Professor of Elocution.

I. Individual Criticism, Vocal Culture, and Expression.

II. From six to ten hours, as my time varies during the different terms of the year.

III. All of my time is devoted to personal drill and criticism.

IV. I do not use text-books in my department as a general thing, for two reasons—first, because the time allotted me for each class is so short, it would be impossible to master any one of them; and, secondly, because there is so much minutia in them, that I consider them impracticable.

V. Original Orations are delivered to me by the Sophomore class during the second term, for criticism.

VI. I give instruction in Elocution to private pupils from the different classes, in addition to my regular duties at the College.

VII. -----

89

VIII. I would respectfully suggest that more time and prominence be given to this department. As it is now, only the shreds of time that remain from the other departments are given to this. The students feel this need as well as myself.

The chief benefit to be derived from Elocutionary instruction, *must* come from close individual drill and criticism ; lectures or *general* criticism cannot meet this want.

More than two-thirds of the students who come to the College, read badly and have undeveloped voices; and no acquirement of technical rules, or lectures can benefit them. It must come to them individually from the teacher by the closest training.

I would suggest that four or five hours daily be allotted me for this training; making individual appointments that will not conflict with other recitations.

IX. I have not published any pamphlet or book during the past year.

JOHN B. McMASTER, A.M., C. E.,

Instructor in Civil Engineering.

I. I am partially in charge, as assistant to Professor Charles McMillan, of the departments of Geodesy and Topographical Drawing, and temporarily in charge of the course of instruction in Descriptive Geometry and Industrial Drawings.

The course in Geodesy embraces instruction in Chain and Compass Surveying, Adjustment of Field Instruments, Leveling, Topographical Surveying, Hydrography, Triangulation, Town Plane Table, and Mine Surveying, preliminary and final survey of routes, and staking out for construction.

Instruction is also given in Pen and Colored Topography, in the preparation of Contour Maps, Hydrographic Charts, Town Maps, Plans and Profiles of Mines, and Maps of Landscape Surveys. For a more detailed statement, I would respectfully refer to the replies of Professor Charles McMillan.

The instruction given in Descriptive Geometry includes a thorough course of Projections, both Plane, Spherical, Axonometric and Oblique ; a course in

Shades and Shadows, Perspective, Trihedrals, and Isometric Drawing. This course is necessary in order to enable the students to begin the preparation of their maps, bridge-drawing, etc.

The course in Industrial Drawing is designed to furnish instruction to the students in the use of a draughtsman's tools and colors; in the representation of all manner of curved surfaces by brush and right line shading, and of wood, brick, stone, earth, water and the metals by means of colors.

II. The hours devoted to instruction in the departments now under my charge amount to twenty-eight and one-half per week. They are divided as follows :

Monday, $4\frac{1}{2}$ hours; Tuesday, $4\frac{1}{2}$ hours; Wednesday, 4 hours; Thursday, $5\frac{1}{2}$ hours; Friday, $6\frac{1}{2}$ hours; Saturday, $3\frac{1}{2}$ hours ; total, 28.5 hours.

III. During the first and third terms, when much of the time is taken up with work in the field, about one-third of the number of hours is devoted to lectures. In the winter, or during the second term, the proportion is about one-half.

IV. The text-books used in my departments are Gillespie's Land Surveying, Gillespie's Higher Land Surveying, Warren's Descriptive Geometry, Warren's Stereotomy, Enthoffer's Topographical Drawing.

V. No written exercises are required from the students under my charge.

VI. Instruction is given to a number of students, at present three, in special courses, such as Geodesy, and Map-Drawing. All students of the regular course in Civil Engineering, are also invited to take as much optional work as they can. This generally fills the hours between twelve and one o'clock, and between two and three o'clock. Some instruction is given at night, such as finding the meridian by the North Star and determining the variation of the needle. Such exercises are optional. The number of hours spent per week amounts at present to six, making the total number of hours of instruction per week, 34.5. I have no private pupils.

VII. Exercises corresponding to Laboratory Work are held, namely : Map Drawing, Topographical Drawing, Industrial Drawing, Stereotomy.

VIII. As assistant to Professor McMillan, I beg to be excused from answering this question.

IX. Have published during the past year—

1. Profiles of High Masonry Dams. (Republished).
2. Hydraulic Mining—Scientific American.
3. Telemetric Measurements.
4. Geometry of Position applied to Surveying. Van Nostrand's Engineering Magazine.
5. The Bad Lands of Wyoming, in the Bulletin of the American Geographical Society, being an address delivered before that Society on February 9th, 1880.
6. Transmission of Power by Compressed Air.
7. Have prepared for the press a text-book on The Geometry of Position.
8. Have also in preparation a text-book on The Anatomy of an Iron Truss Railway Bridge.

MALCOM McNEILL, A.B.,

Assistant in Astronomy.

I am Assistant in Astronomy. My work is almost wholly at the observatory. I have no recitations or lectures. I assist in giving instruction to the class in Practical Astronomy—teaching the use of instruments and superintending and assisting them in their observations and computations. I also assist Professor Young in the lecture room when there is any need. My work with the class takes two or three hours on almost every clear evening. I also assist Professor Young in any observations he may be making, and do most of the computing.

I assisted in reducing some observations on the "Diameter of Mars," the results of which were published in the Astronomische Nachrichten. I made the reductions of a series of comet observations taken partly by Professor Young, and partly by myself. I made most of the computation for the Longitude of the observatory, and am at present engaged in making an accurate computation of its Latitude.

94

WILLIAM F. MAGIE, A.B.,

Assistant in Physics.

Acting as I do, as Prof. Brackett's assistant, I am engaged in all his laboratory work, besides aiding in the experiments shown to the Juniors, and to some extent in their instruction, and in the instruction of the Senior classes in practical laboratory work. I have no special students and give no instruction outside of the laboratory hours.